Encountering

Through

Tables, Charts and Art

Encountering the Past

Through

Tables, Charts and Art

John Soares

West/Wadsworth
I(T)P® An International Thomson Publishing Company

Belmont, CA • Albany, NY • Boston • Cincinnati • Johannesburg
London • Madrid • Melbourne • Mexico City • New York
Pacific Grove, CA • Scottsdale, AZ • Singapore • Tokyo • Toronto

Printed in the United States of America 1 2 3 4 5 6 7 8 9 10

For more information, contact Wadsworth Publishing Company,
10 Davis Drive, Belmont, CA 94002, or electronically at
http://www.thomson.com/wadsworth.html

International Thomson
Publishing Europe
Berkshire House
168-173 High Holborn
London, WC1V 7AA, United Kingdom

International Thomson
Editores
Seneca, 53
Colonia Polanco
11560 México D.F. México

Nelson ITP, Australia
102 Dodds Street
South Melbourne
Victoria 3205 Australia

International Thomson
Publishing Asia
60 Albert Street #15-01
Albert Complex
Singapore 189969

Nelson Canada
Birchmount Road
Scarborough, Ontario
Canada M1K 5G4

International Thomson 1120
Publishing Japan
Hirakawa-cho Kyowa bldg 3F
2-2-1 Hirakawa-cho,
Chiyoda-ku, Tokyo 102, Japan

International Thomson
Publishing Southern Africa
Building 18, Constantia Square
138 Sixteenth Road, P.O. Box 2459
Halfway House, 1685 South Africa

Senior Developmental Editor-Sharon Adams Poore
Print Buyer-Stacey Weinberger
Editorial Assistant-Melissa Gleason
Ancillary Coordinator-Rita Jaramillo

ISBN 0-534-54555-6

CONTENTS

Encountering the Past

Through

Tables, Charts and Art

INTRODUCTION

This supplement is designed to augment your history learning experience. It does so by helping you explore the meaning and interpretation of all the numerous tables and charts so generously distributed throughout the text, and also by doing the same for one illustration per chapter.

UNDERSTANDING TABLES AND CHARTS

One of the many strengths of *Western Civilization* is the inclusion of these tables and charts, which bring greater understanding to the material through concrete numbers that cover everything from the living conditions of serfs to the exorbitant excesses of monarchs to the millions of dead in World Wars I and II.

For each text chapter you'll find an explanation for all tables and charts, along with two or more questions about each. The questions require you to carefully examine and interpret the data, and in some cases make mathematical calculations, usually of the basic-math variety, although there are a few questions that require basic algebra. So yes, you'll probably want a calculator. Note that quantification can be very useful, but be aware that much of the data, especially from periods prior to the twentieth century, can be incomplete or inaccurate.

Your goal is to understand what the table or chart conveys. Here's how to best do that:

- Begin by reading the title caption, which gives a broad indication of the subject of the graphic.

- Next examine the labels on the rows and columns on tables, and the titles on the y- and x-axes (vertical and horizontal portions) of graphs; this gives you a clearer understanding of what countries, groups, years, etc. are being described.

- Then look at the data in detail. What overall patterns do you see? How clear are they? Are there differences between countries or groups? If so, how large? You should be able to give a one- or two-sentence summary of the main information in the graphic.

- Ask yourself how reliable the data is. Look at the bottom for the source or sources. Ask yourself how they obtained the data, and how well that data might accord with reality.

- Also ask yourself what is left out of the graphic, and what else would be useful to gain a better understanding of the graphic's subject.

Bear in mind that there often is not a precise answer to the questions: You'll have to use your best judgment or make inferences. Also, some questions ask you to apply the data to the larger context of the chapter's material and/or speculate on possible causes, conditions, or future events. Through the process of answering the questions you'll learn to think like a historian.

WHERE DID THE DATA COME FROM?

The oldest data for hunting and gathering groups, and some of the data from the early periods of expanding civilization, comes through the methods of archaeology. Archaeology often begins with a carefully conducted excavation of an archaeological site, followed by analysis of what is found. (See Table 1.1 for an example.) Dates of artifact creation are determined through several methods, or a combination of methods; examples include tree-ring dating, radioactive dating, examination of sequential layers of sediment deposits (stratigraphy), and chemical analysis of bone.

As the centuries passed, more and more data was collected. The most important source of such data has been government. In many areas the government, either for the entire realm or at the local level, began conducting censuses of the population. Government also began keeping records of births and deaths, and classifying people by profession, etc. Governments also kept financial records, especially at the macro-economic level, so we have substantial data on government spending, sources of revenue, and government debt. And it also makes sense that governments would know how many people were in the army, and also how many were killed or wounded in a battle. Over time the number of statistics and their completeness grew substantially; you'll find that the latter chapters covering the period from about the eighteenth century onward have far more tables than the preceding chapters.

There are other sources of data. Churches sometimes kept records on their members. Businesses also keep records of their financial transactions, such as what they sold and for how much, and how much they paid workers. Finally, individual households, especially those of the upper class, kept various records.

ART INTERPRETATION AND APPRECIATION

For each text chapter you'll find a series of questions about one illustration, along with occasional comments. Many of the illustrations are paintings; a few are sculptures or line drawings or photos, the latter two intended to illustrate important aspects of time and place and custom rather than to be solely works of art.

The art we discuss stretches across a span of 25,000 or so years and encompasses many styles and subjects. If you are an artist or have a strong background in art, you'll feel right at home. If you don't, here are the main aspects of art to examine:

- Line gives the shape to the objects in a picture.
- Color has a primary appeal to the senses and can be very effective at stimulating emotions.
- Light, specifically the use of lighter and darker areas, can direct attention to certain areas and can also stimulate emotions.
- Composition refers to the size and placement of objects.
- Meaning—what message or mood was the artist seeking to convey?

PART ONE: THE ANCIENT WORLD

CHAPTER ONE
PREHISTORIC EUROPE AND THE NEOLITHIC REVOLUTION

TABLE ANALYSIS

Table 1.1: The Domestication of Animals (p. 9)

This table provides data on the number and types of animal bones found at three different Neolithic sites in central Europe during the time period from about 3200 B.C. through about 2400 B.C. Scientists recovered bones from four types of domestic animals and six types of wild animals. By counting the number of bones from each type of animal, the researchers were able to determine its percentage of the total by dividing that number by the total number of bones. The data indicates the dependence these three cultures had already developed on domestic animals: Bones from domestic animals outnumber those of wild animals by at least four to one.

Question 1: Compare the percentage of domestic animal bones found at the Tarnabod site with those of the other two sites. Is it possible to draw a conclusion about changing levels of reliance on domestic animals over time? What sources of error do you think could arise in finding and counting the bones?

Question 2: What factors could have caused the aurochs to become extinct? Does the data give any indication as to when aurochs numbers began to decline in Central Europe? Do you think there could be a correlation between the numbers of wild game animals available and changes in the use of domestic animals?

ART INTERPRETATION

Illustration 1.2: The Willendorf Venus (p. 9)

This small limestone statue, about four inches high, was found in a loess deposit in Austria in 1908. Stratigraphic dating (based on position within a series of sequential layers—strata—of sediment deposits) and radioactive dating give a range of dates of origin from 30,000 B.C. to 20,000 B.C. She was created by a member of a nomadic tribe of hunter gatherers, possibly as a symbol of fertility or as a representation of a goddess, or as a good luck charm for hunters in the field.

Questions to ponder:

1. What features of the statue suggest fertility?

2. What could be the significance of the obesity of the figure, assuming that the hunter-gatherer lifestyle and caloric intake probably did not allow for obesity in many people?

3. What could be the significance of the lack of facial features?

4. If this statue was a religious object, what could you infer about the nature of the religion?

5. How does the body shape of the figurine compare with the female body shape now considered ideal in western society?

CHAPTER TWO
THE ANCIENT NEAR EAST: MESOPOTAMIA, EGYPT, PHOENICIA, ISRAEL

TABLE ANALYSIS

There are no tables in this chapter.

ART INTERPRETATION

Illustration 2.7: The Pharaoh Menkaure and His Queen (p. 31)

Menkaure was an Old Kingdom Pharaoh. His pyramid is the third largest at Giza and was built just after the two largest ones.

Questions to ponder:

1. What do the clothes the pair is wearing indicate about Egypt's climate?

2. What could be the possible meaning of the headdress worn by the Pharaoh?

3. Look at Menkaure's physique. Do you think he actually looked like that, or is it possible the sculptor was under orders to make him look like that?

4. The queen is embracing Menkaure, not the other way around. What could be the significance of this?

CHAPTER THREE
ANCIENT GREECE TO THE END OF THE PELOPONNESIAN WAR

TABLE ANALYSIS

Table 3.1: Cities of the Ancient World (p. 53)

This table gives population estimates for the largest cities of the Mediterranean and Near East regions in 430 B.C. Note that the numbers are approximate, usually rounded to the nearest 5000, or, in the case of Carthage and Persepolis, as a range.

Question 1: Where are the two largest cities located? Why do you think this region had large cities, whereas the population of Greece was apportioned among many smaller cities?

Question 2: In what ways could a large population give a city/country more power than a city/country with a smaller population?

Question 3: What reasons could account for Carthage and Persepolis populations being given as a range rather than as a rounded number?

ART INTERPRETATION

Illustration 3.5: Hoplite Warfare (p. 54)

Questions to ponder:

1. Examine the armor and protection of the hoplite soldiers. What parts of their bodies are least protected?

2. Why were arrows relatively ineffective against hoplite soldiers?

3. Hoplite soldiers wore relatively heavy armor. Why would such armor be an advantage when fighting in a phalanx, but perhaps not when fighting in the open, outside of a phalanx?

4. Hoplite soldiers gained some power within the polis. Does it make sense for a country to allow its soldiers to participate in decision-making? Would they perhaps be less likely to support war? Does justice require that they be allowed to participate in decisions that could result in their death or injury?

CHAPTER FOUR
GREEK CULTURE AND ITS HELLENISTIC DIFFUSION

TABLE ANALYSIS

There are no tables in this chapter.

Part One

ART INTERPRETATION

Illustration 4.2 The Parthenon, Athens (p. 77)

This famous temple was built to house a 40-foot statue of Athena, the goddess after whom the city of Athens was named. The ivory and gold statue has been gone for many centuries. The Parthenon served a variety of religious functions: In addition to being a Greek temple, it was also a Christian church, and, during the period Greece was controlled by the Ottoman Empire, a mosque. The Ottomans were at war with the Venetians in 1687 when the Venetians launched a rocket at an Ottoman ammunition dump in the Parthenon, destroying the central portion of the monument.

Questions to ponder:

1. The architects designed the Doric columns of the Parthenon so that they gradually thinned toward the top. This was done to overcome parallax, the illusion of the human eye that rising columns (or buildings) are not parallel to each other, even though they actually are. How well did the builders do their job?

2. The Parthenon had a roof, but no walls. In which seasons do you think the lack of walls would be an advantage? In which seasons would the lack of walls be a disadvantage?

3. Britain removed the statues from the Parthenon and now exhibits them in the British Museum. Should the British return them to Greece?

CHAPTER FIVE
THE RISE OF THE ROMAN REPUBLIC

TABLE ANALYSIS

Table 5.1 The Servian Classification of Male Citizens (p. 112)

This table presents numbers of men in the Roman military, broken down into eight categories based on the amount of wealth owned by the individuals in each class. The wealth is approximated in *asses*, a type of coin introduced in the century following the census that classified these troops in 444 B.C. The cavalry consisted of patricians. The classes were ranked one through five in order of descending wealth. The Roman government categorized men into groups of 100, called a century.

Question 1: Which class is the most numerous? Least numerous?

Question 2: Compare the number of men in the cavalry and Class I with the combined total of the others. What does this say about the relative power of the two groups?

Question 3: Why are the property qualification numbers only estimates?

Question 4: What would be the advantages and disadvantages of having members of the same class fight side by side?

ART INTERPRETATION

Illustration 5.6: A Census (p. 112)

Questions to ponder:

1. What classes of citizens are present?

2. What inferences can you make about Roman religion?

3. How does the illustration depict both the functioning of government (scribe, assessor, soldiers) and the attitudes of the citizenry toward the government?

4. What are the primary reasons for the conducting of censuses in western countries today? How do these reasons differ from the reasons for the Roman census?

CHAPTER SIX
SOCIAL, POLITICAL, AND ECONOMIC STRUCTURES OF IMPERIAL ROME

TABLE ANALYSIS

Table 6.1: Citizenship in the Roman Republic, 264-70 B.C (p. 131)

This table presents estimates of the number of adult male citizens for a nearly 200-year period in the Roman republic. The numbers change substantially, in part due to changing rules as to who could be a citizen and also as the number of total people under the control of Rome changed. This latter figure shifted after war gains and losses.

Question 1: In which year was the population of the Republic highest? Lowest? How can you account for the large difference between these two numbers?

Question 2: Around approximately what year was the rate of population change the greatest? (Hint: Make a graph, with population on the y axis and year on the x axis.)

Question 3: What are all the factors that could conceivably affect the population estimates?

Table 6.2: Roman Wages and Prices in the Late Republic (p. 140)

This table gives estimates of wages for slaves, free laborers, and soldiers, and also estimates of the prices of food, clothes, slaves, and animals for c. 150 B.C. By examining the data and performing elementary math, it is possible to determine how long members of the three classes would have to work to purchase the various items.

Question 1: The text describes the second century B.C. as a time of "economic polarization" in the Republic. What parts of the data in the table tend to support this observation?

Question 2: If a free laborer were able to obtain five days employment per week for 50 weeks a year, how much more or less money would he make in a year than a soldier would for the same time period?

Question 3: Ignoring the costs of feeding, clothing, and housing, how many days would a patrician have to hire out his farm slave as unskilled labor before he would regain the purchase price of the slave?
Question 4: What could explain why the price of wheat was lower in regions farther from Rome?

ART INTERPRETATION

Illustration 6.4: Augustus as Princeps (p. 134)

Questions to ponder:

1. What could be the significance of the small figure near Augustus's right calf?

2. Based on his clothes, what inferences can you make about Augustus and the image portrayed of Augustus by the sculptor?

3. What could be the significance of the position of Augustus's right arm and hand?

PART TWO: THE MIDDLE AGES

CHAPTER SEVEN
THE ORIGINS OF CHRISTIANITY AND THE DECLINE OF THE ROMAN EMPIRE

TABLE ANALYSIS

Table 7.1: The Population of the Roman Empire, A.D. 1-600 (p. 163)

This table gives population estimates at 200-year intervals for the various parts of the Roman Empire from A.D. 1 through 600 A.D. The data demonstrates an increase for the first 200 years, followed by substantial decline as the Empire weakened and disintegrated.

Question 1: Which part of the Empire experienced the greatest population decrease as a percentage between 200 A.D. and 600 A.D.? Which experienced the smallest decrease?

Question 2: What factors account for the declining population in the provinces?

Question 3: Why can the decrease in population of the Empire be correlated with the declining strength of the Empire? In what ways can population changes of an empire affect its power?

ART INTERPRETATION

Illustration 7.8 The Arch of Constantine (p. 170)

Questions to ponder:

1. What reasons would Constantine have for erecting the arch?

2. Why would Constantine include past emperors on the arch?

3. Describe the activities depicted on the arch. What is the overall theme of the arch?

4. How do you think members of the various classes viewed the arch?

CHAPTER EIGHT
ROME'S SUCCESSORS: BYZANTIUM, ISLAM, AND THE GERMANIC WEST

TABLE ANALYSIS

There are no tables in this chapter.

ART INTERPRETATION

Illustration 8.4: The Dome of the Rock, Jerusalem (p. 191)

A masterpiece of Moslem architecture, the Dome of the Rock is built on a site that is sacred to both Jews and Moslems. For Jews the entire area is the remains of Solomon's Temple; at the nearby Wailing Wall devout Jews come daily to pray and place notes to God in the wall's cracks. The Dome of the Rock itself surrounds a rock from which the prophet Mohammed journeyed to heaven with the angel Gabriel, making it one of the most holy sites in Islam.

Questions to ponder:

1. From a geographical perspective, why is the Dome of the Rock an item of contention between Jews and Moslems?

2. What aspects of the Dome of the Rock demonstrate Byzantine influences?

3. The Dome of the Rock is situated in the Old City of Jerusalem, an area under the control of Israel since it was captured in a war in 1967 from Jordan. Currently the Israeli government controls access to the mosque. Should it continue to do so, or should it allow Moslems unrestricted access to the site? What reasons can you give to

support the policy of the Israeli government? What arguments can you give for unrestricted access?

CHAPTER NINE
THE BEGINNINGS OF THE FEUDAL AGE

TABLE ANALYSIS

There are no tables in this chapter.

ART INTERPRETATION

Illustration 9.7 Detail from the Bayeux Tapestry (p. 220)

The Bayeux Tapestry depicts the Norman invasion of Anglo-Saxon England in 1066. An example of Romanesque art, it has flat characters on a neutral background. Despite this, it gives realistic depictions of men, animals, boats, and weapons, and well conveys the sense of action. Consisting of linen with wool embroidering, and constructed over a roughly ten-year period beginning in 1070, it is of great use to historians since it was created shortly after the event it depicts and is thus more likely to give accurate depictions than works of art created long after eye-witnesses are dead.

Questions to ponder:

1. In what ways is the Bayeux Tapestry analogous to films of the Vietnam War and World War II?

2. In what language are the words on the tapestry written? What do you think they might say?

3. What aspects of the tapestry demonstrate the Viking heritage of the Normans?

4. Examine the Viking-style boats. How seaworthy do they look? How fast do you think they could go under sail power compared to modern sailing vessels?

5. What could be the significance of the creatures depicted along the bottom of the tapestry?

CHAPTER TEN
MEDIEVAL RELIGION AND THOUGHT

TABLE ANALYSIS

There are no tables in this chapter.

ART INTERPRETATION

Illustration 10.3 Reims Cathedral (p. 238)

Reims cathedral is the quintessential example of the complexity and detail of the High Gothic architectural style. Its numerous pinnacles draw the eye upward toward heaven. It is also notable for the numerous sculpted figures adorning the walls.

Questions to ponder:

1. What do you think would be the difficulties in constructing this cathedral? What hazards would the workers face?

2. Many of the medieval cathedrals were designed to impress the masses with the glory of God. How do you think the poor viewed these edifices? Do you think it instilled them with Holy Spirit, or did some think about all the food and clothing that could have been purchased with the construction money?

3. In what ways do the architectural features of Reims Cathedral differ with those of the Abbey of St. Leger in Illustration 10.2 on page 237, a structure built in the Romanesque style?

CHAPTER ELEVEN
ECONOMIC DEVELOPMENT AND URBAN GROWTH IN THE HIGH MIDDLE AGES

TABLE ANALYSIS

Table 11.1: Population Changes in Medieval Europe (p. 262)

This table lists population estimates for various regions of Europe for five different years from 500 A.D. through 1450 A.D. The collapse of the Roman Empire brought substantial declines in population across Europe. These losses were recovered and exceeded by 1000 A.D. The population expanded significantly with the agricultural revolution to peak levels in 1340 A.D. The Black Death then ravaged Europe, causing a major drop in population numbers that was still far from 1340 levels even 110 years later in 1450 A.D.

Question 1: Which region had the greatest percentage population decline from 1340 to 1450? Which region had the smallest?

Question 2: What possible reasons can you give to explain why some regions suffered greater percentage losses from the Black Death than did other regions?

Question 3: The text states that agricultural productivity doubled between 1000 and 1250. Do the population figures provide support for this assertion?

Question 4: Outside of the Slavic areas, which region had the greatest percentage population increase between 500 and 1340? Which region had the smallest percentage population increase during the same time span? What possible explanations can you give to explain the difference between the two regions?

Table 11.2: Medieval Grain Yields (p. 265)

This table gives data on grain yields on an estate in Winchester, England for a 140-year period beginning in 1209 and ending in 1349. Yields of three grains—barley, oats, and wheat—are measured in both grains per grain planted and in bushels per acre, with maximum and minimum values given for each.

Question 1: Which grain gave the highest yield in grains per grain planted? Bushels per acre?

Question 2: Which grain gave the lowest yield in grains per grain planted? Bushels per acre?

Question 3: Why would the estate planners grow the lower producing grains?

Question 4: What methods of modern agriculture have made much higher grain yields possible?

Table 11.3 : Urban Populations Before the Black Death (p. 271)

This table gives estimated populations for 23 urban areas in Europe in the 1250-1300 time period. None had populations significantly greater than 100,000; most were much smaller.

Question 1: What qualities of Milan, Venice, and Florence resulted in their being the largest cities in Europe around 1250?

Question 2: Why do you think German cities tended to be smaller on average than cities in Italy?

Question 3: What factors help explain why no cities reached populations greater than 100,000? What factors help explain why modern cities can reach 10 million or more?

ART INTERPRETATION

Illustration 11.10 An Urban Street Scene in Fourteenth-Century Siena (p. 277)

Questions to ponder:

1. List the occupations in which people in the illustration are engaged.

2. Note the ground floor openings and the windows. Do you think they would be of a different size and type in Northern Europe? Why?

3. Several people are transporting things. What are the different ways they are accomplishing the task?

4. None of the buildings rise higher than a few stories. Why do you think this was so?

5. Look at the construction workers in the upper left portion of the illustration. How would that type of construction be done today?

CHAPTER TWELVE
MATERIAL AND SOCIAL LIFE IN THE MIDDLE AGES

TABLE ANALYSIS

Table 12.1: Wages and Earnings in Thirteenth-Century England (p. 286)

This table give information on estimated earnings for a variety of professions in thirteen-century England. Earnings are given in the coinage system in use at the time, with twelve pennies to a shilling and twenty shillings to a pound. There is a substantial earnings difference among the various professions, with agricultural laborers paid the lowest amount and skilled laborers the highest. Use the data in this table in conjunction with Table 12.2 to gain a better understanding of how long laborers had to work to obtain food and supplies; this allows you to make an approximation of the standard of living of the lower classes at that time.

Question 1: Assuming a 250-day work year, who had a higher average annual income, a mason or a town priest?

Question 2: Since we're looking at that town priest, why do you think he received so much more money than a rural priest?

Question 3: What could be the reasons why a royal huntsman was paid more than a carpenter?

Question 4: The table's caption states that wages increased 40 to 50 percent after the Black Death. Why do you think this happened? (Hint: What is one of the fundamental concepts of economics?)

Question 5: Of the professions listed, which would you prefer to practice if you lived in that time? Why?

Question 6: If you had to break up the laborers in the table into classes, which laborers would go into what classes? What is your rationale for creating the classes? Are you using strictly economic criteria, or do you think a profession such as the priesthood should be considered a separate class, regardless of income?

Table 12.2 Prices in Thirteenth-Century England (p. 286)

The values listed in this table are only estimates, since the supply and thus the price of the various goods could shift dramatically based on natural factors such as weather and climate, and also on human factors such as government policies and wars. Prices are given in the same units as in Table 12.1. Use Table 12.1 to gain an understanding of the standard of living for the various laborers listed in Table 12.1.

Question 1: Assume a mason has a wife and four children. Estimate how much this family would spend on food in a month if they ate only bread, eggs, and hens. How much would they have left over at the end of the month for housing, clothing, and other necessities? Use Table 12.1 for income data and make your best guesses on food consumption.

Question 2: Given that the wages and prices and monthly food intake for Question 1 are only estimates, do you see the difficulty in getting precise numbers with a definite meaning when dealing with this type of data? If you have a science background you are familiar with uncertainty estimates for measured values. Imagine how high the uncertainty must be for the number you calculated in Question 1.

Question 3: Why would pepper be so much more expensive than bread?

Table 12.3: The Relative Weight of Cattle (p. 287)

This table compares the weight in pounds of cattle of various ages, ranging from 5 months to 5 years, for the same region in Italy for both the seventeenth century and the twentieth century. The twentieth century values are three to three-and-a-half times higher, due in large part to improved breeding and feeding of the cattle.

Question 1: Which cow probably had the most fat as a percentage of body weight, the seventeenth-century cow or the twentieth-century cow?

Question 2: Consider a peasant family in this region in the seventeenth century with twenty acres of land, and also consider a present-day family in the same region with twenty acres of land. Which would be most likely to slaughter a cow when the cow was younger? Why?

Table 12.4: Life Expectancy in the Middle Ages (p. 290)

This table presents the estimated life expectancy of male landholders in England for several time spans, beginning in 1200 and ending in 1450, and for the ages 0, 10, 20, 30, 40, 60, and 80 years. The values give the estimate of the number of years a person would live, on average, upon reaching that age.

Question 1: What reasons help explain why the life expectancy at age 10 is greater than that at age 0?

Question 2: Do you think these numbers are higher or lower than those for males who did not own land? Why?

Question 3: Which age has the highest life expectancy? How do you explain this?

Question 4: What is the trend of the life expectancy for newborns over the time period studied? How can you account for it?

Question 5: If you were a thirty-year-old male landholder in England in the year 1300, would the life expectancy of your children encourage you to have more or less of them? What factors would influence your opinion? If you were the wife of that landholder, do you think you would necessarily share the opinion of your husband? Why or why not?

Table 12.5: The Expenses of the Rich (p. 297)

This table presents data on the prices of various items common to the lifestyle of the rich of thirteenth-century England. See Tables 12.1 and 12.2 for comparisons of the incomes of lower classes and the goods they commonly purchased, and also for the values of English currency.

Question 1: Why were the spices so expensive?

Question 2: Of all the items listed, which would you classify as essential? Helpful? Pure extravagance?

Question 3: The 1000 pounds minimum spent by a nobleman would have paid the wages of how many masons? (See Table 12.1)

Table 12.6 Average Age of Women at First Marriage (p. 303)

This table gives figures on the average age of women entering their first marriage. There is data from several locations in both southern and northern Europe, and several time periods, the earliest beginning in 1451, the latest ending in 1719. There is a substantial disparity across time and space.

Question 1: What reasons can you give for women marrying in their teens in fifteenth-century Florence and in their mid- to later twenties in seventeenth-century Amsterdam?

Question 2: Which time period and region had the lowest marriage age? Which had the highest?

Question 3: In what ways could the economic status of the family of a young single woman affect the age at which she would marry?

Part Two

ART INTERPRETATION

Illustration 12.6: The Ordination of a Knight (p. 294)

Questions to ponder:

1. Note the woman in the right foreground. What is the significance of the weapons she carries? What do you think the lettering on the scabbard refers to?

2. Where do you think this ceremony is taking place?

3. Do you think the mixing of religion with the knighting process strengthened or weakened monarchy? What about the power of the church?

4. What do you think is the profession of the men standing at right?

PART THREE: EARLY MODERN EUROPE

CHAPTER THIRTEEN
PLAGUE, WAR, AND SOCIAL CHANGE IN THE "LONG" FOURTEENTH CENTURY

TABLE ANALYSIS

Table 13.1: Indices of Population Increase in Europe, 1000-1950 (p. 312)

This table presents nearly 1000 years of population estimates. The estimates are based as a percentage of the estimated population in the year 1000 and are presented as a bar chart in 50-year increments, with the index on the y-axis and the 50-year increments on the x-axis.

Question 1: The caption for the illustration states that the estimates on which the data is based are controversial. What could be the reason(s) for this controversy?

Question 2: What do you think are the major causes of the substantial population decrease between 1900 and 1950?

Question 3: What time period had the lowest index value? The highest?

Question 4: Based on the difference between the highest and lowest index values, which 150-year period saw the greatest change in population, either up or down? How can you explain this population change?

Table 13.2: Population, Prices, and Wages in England, 1300-1500 (p. 314)

This table depicts estimated changes in three variables—agriculture prices, industrial wages, and population—for the time period 1300 to 1500 in England. All values are given as a percentage relative to the value in 1300. Note that for much of the time period, wages were higher relative to 1300 values than were agricultural prices.

Question 1: By looking at the graph, can you infer the major cause of wage increases between about 1340 and 1380?

Question 2: Examine the time period from 1520 to 1550. What factors could explain the rise in both wages and agriculture prices? Could change in one variable have affected the other? Why?

Question 3: What are the maximum and minimum values for population, agricultural prices, and industrial wages?

ART INTERPRETATION

Illustration 13.10: Detail from the *Ghent Altarpiece* (p. 334)

The *Ghent Altarpiece*, the quintessential example of early Flemish painting, was created between 1425 and 1432 by the Flemish painter Jan Van Eyck. The entire work contains twenty pieces of different shapes and sizes, each a different scene, most depicting major events and people in Christianity. The detail in the illustration is only a portion of one of the smallest panels. The entire altar piece is eleven feet high and fourteen feet long.

Questions to ponder:

1. What could be the significance of this scene being on the altarpiece, and in a church in general?

2. How realistic are the colors and the depiction of objects and people?

3. In what ways do the clothing, horses, and various accouterments denote the social class of the people depicted?

4. Do the facial expressions give you any idea as to what the riders are supposedly thinking about the task ahead of them?

CHAPTER FOURTEEN
THE RENAISSANCE: POLITICAL RENEWAL AND INTELLECTUAL CHANGE

TABLE ANALYSIS

There are no tables in this chapter.

ART INTERPRETATION

Illustration 14.8: *The Birth of Venus* by Botticelli (p. 259)

Sandro Botticelli created this painting around 1486 by blending elements of Gothic art styles common in Europe at the time with themes from Roman times. He modeled Venus after a statue of the goddess from Roman times, the *Medici Venus*.

Questions to ponder:

1. What aspects of the painting depict the emergence-from-the-sea aspect of Venus' birth?

2. Why is the couple on the left in the picture? What does the male appear to be doing?

3. The painting breaks with the common depiction of Christian themes to present a scene from an ancient pagan religion. Why did Botticelli feel he could do so?

CHAPTER FIFTEEN
THE RELIGIOUS REFORMATIONS OF THE SIXTEENTH CENTURY

TABLE ANALYSIS

There are no tables in this chapter.

ART INTERPRETATION

Illustration 15.8: The Final Session of the Council of Trent, 1563 (p. 381)

Titian, the anglicized name of the Venetian Tiziano Vecelli, was born around 1490 and died in 1576. Considered the father of modern painting, he pioneered the use of rough-textured canvas for paintings and is well-known for his use of color.

Questions to ponder:

1. Who are the men seated in benches with the large white hats? Do you think they see the people in the front very well? Can you imagine seeing a movie in a theater if everyone wore such large hats?

2. Who are the gentlemen in front? Do you think this was a democratic gathering, or that full and free dissent and debate were encouraged?

3. What kind of building is this? Can you imagine what it would feel like to spend an entire cold winter day sitting on a hard bench in it?

4. What reasons could there be for soldiers at the Council of Trent? Who would the Catholic Church fear?

CHAPTER SIXTEEN
OVERSEAS CONQUEST AND RELIGIOUS WAR TO 1648

TABLE ANALYSIS

Table 16.1: Population Decline in Central Mexico (p. 397)

This table gives population range estimates of various sections of Central Mexico for the period 1530-35 and the year 1568. In all cases except Tlaxcala, mortality exceeded 50 percent.

Question 1: What would be the difficulties in establishing accurate population and mortality data for this time and place?

Question 2: Which area had the greatest percentage decrease in population?

Question 3: Why do you think the population of Tlaxcala did not suffer any significant population decline?

Question 4: How can you explain the different mortality rates for the two sectors of West Puebla?

Table 16.2 Crown Income and Debt in Castile (p. 415)

This table provides data on the annual revenue, total accumulated debt, and the amount of annual interest paid on that total accumulated debt for six years spanning a time period from 1515 to 1667 in Castile.

Question 1: Calculate the interest rate charged on the accumulated debt for each of the six years. Was it the same for all years? Why would it change?

Question 2: What year had the lowest accumulated debt-to-revenue ratio? Which had the highest? How do you think an ever-increasing debt affects the long-term foreign and domestic health of a country?

Question 3: The caption states that Castile spent nearly 90 percent of its revenue on defense. By contrast, most European countries today spend less than ten percent of revenue on the military. How can you account for the drastic change in priorities? (Hint: Examine why modern Euro-pean countries need a military, and the degree of influence the general population has on government.)

ART INTERPRETATION

Illustration 16.6: Charles V (p. 401)

Questions to ponder:

1. Examine the armor on the emperor. How well does it protect him?

2. Note the protection for the horse. Why is it necessary?

3. How much do you think a cavalry man valued a well-trained horse as opposed to one that was spirited?

4. Do you think Charles V commissioned this portrait? What would indicate a commissioned portrait?

CHAPTER SEVENTEEN
PRE-INDUSTRIAL EUROPE: SCIENCE, THE ECONOMY, AND POLITICAL REORGANIZATION

TABLE ANALYSIS

Table 17.1: English Trade Balances (p. 437)

This table gives numbers for England's trade balance, as a whole and outside Europe, for ten different times during the period 1699 to 1711, an era that saw much war in Europe. A country's trade balance is posi-tive when the value of its exports is greater than the value of its imports.

Question 1: Why would a larger positive trade balance for a country tend to decrease its unemployment?

Question 2: What factors could affect the extra-European trade balance?

Question 3: For the period 1702 to 1711, which year had the largest overall trade balance and which had the least? What factors could help account for these findings?

Question 4: How could a positive trade balance lead to increased power for a country, in both economic and military terms?

Table 17.2: English Wages and Prices, 1541-1702 (p. 440)

This table presents estimated average weekly wages for English carpen-ters, farm laborers, and masons for three different time periods in the sixteenth and seventeenth centuries. There are twelve pennies to a shilling and twenty shillings to a pound.

Question 1: Compare the values given in this table with those found in Table 12.1 on page 286. Did wages fall or rise over this larger time period?

Question 2: Of the six types of food, which had the greatest increase in price? The least? How do you think these relative price increases affected the consumption of these items?

Question 3: Why do you think wages did not keep up with inflation for this time period in England? (Hint: How do workers typically manage such a feat in modern European countries?)

Table 17.3: English Incomes, 1688 (p. 440)

This table presents estimates of numbers of families and income in millions of pounds sterling for six different classes in England in 1688. For each class it also gives the percentage of families in that class and their percentage of the total income. By comparing these latter two figures, we can determine the degree of income inequality among the classes. If there were no income inequality, the percentage of families in a class would equal the percentage of total income for that class.

Question 1: How do you think the degree of income inequality affects the stability of a country? If the rich are very rich, and the poor are very poor, are the poor more likely to revolt than if they had a larger share of the country's economic output? What other factors could affect how citizens view the fairness of an economic system?

Question 2: What is the ratio of the number of pounds per family per year in the richest class to the number of pounds per family per year in the poorest class?

Question 3: Regarding annual income, were merchants and traders closer to the next higher class or the next lower class?

ART INTERPRETATION

Illustration 17.8 Louis XIV (p. 432)

Hyacinthe Rigaud (1659-1743) painted *Portrait of Louis XIV* in 1701. Influenced by Flemish artists, Rigaud is well known for portraits; this is his most famous.

Questions to ponder:

1. This portrait was designed to portray Louis in a highly favorable light. What aspects of the painting do you think make the king look like someone ordained by God to rule over millions?

2. Notice the way the king exposes his legs to mid-thigh. Can you imagine any modern European head of state posing in such a manner? What other aspects of the painting demonstrate the vanity of the aging monarch?

3. What is Louis holding in his right hand? What is its significance?

PART FOUR: MODERN EUROPE IN THE AGE OF AGRICULTURAL SOCIETY, 1715-1815

CHAPTER EIGHTEEN
THE SOCIAL AND ECONOMIC STRUCTURE OF THE OLD REGIME

TABLE ANALYSIS

Table 18.1: Estimated Population of Europe in 1700 (p. 448)

This table gives the estimated population in millions for several countries and empires in Europe in the year 1700. Note that the described German and Italian states were independent at this time.

Question 1: Why might it make sense to combine the populations of Sweden and Finland in the year 1700?

Question 2: Which country, empire, or ethnic grouping of countries had the largest population? How do you think this large population affected its power?

Question 3: Compare the population sizes of Spain and Portugal. Does this help explain why Spain eventually overshadowed Portugal?

Table 18.2: The Social Structure of Three French Villages (p. 452)

This table presents income data on 11 classes found in three villages in eastern France in the late eighteenth century. Each occupational class is further broken down as to whether its income would classify it as rich, well-to-do, middling, or poor.

Question 1: Which class had the highest percentage of its members in the poor category? Why do you think this was so?

Question 2: Which class had the highest percentage of its members in the middling category? Why do you think this was so?

Question 3: How many households were categorized as poor? Middling? Well-to-do? Rich? (Hint: You need to use the number of households in a given group, the percentage of the given category in that group, and the total number of households in the three villages.)

Table 18.3 The Social Structure of England in the Old Regime
(p. 453)

This table uses data from late seventeenth-century English tax rolls to develop a social structure of England at that time. The compiler and interpreter of the data gathered information on the total population of England and examined the tax rolls, making logical classifications based on social class.

Question 1: Do you approve of the way this social structure is constructed? Is there a better way to do it that would be more informative or would demonstrate different aspects of English society?

Question 2: What is the average household size?

Question 3: What was the total population of England at that time? Where did the majority live?

Question 4: What percentage of the population was categorized as either rural poor or laborers? What percentage was either aristocracy or land-owning gentry?

Question 5: Excluding the military, 1.3 percent of the population worked in government service. In modern western societies that figure is much higher. What does that say about the level of government services now as opposed to then?

Table 18.4: The Finances of a Great Noble in the Eighteenth Century (p. 455)

This table presents data on income and expenses for the Tavannes, a French noble family, for several time periods between 1696 and 1788. Values are in livres, which had the same approximate value as an English shilling. Note that these records are incomplete for the nearly one-century span, but they do give an indication of the family's finances.

Question 1: Why would the king pay a pension to the Tavannes family?

Question 2: Compare the total capital inherited by the countessi in 1725 with the gross revenue from all land in 1788. How substantial was that inheritance? Was it a significant addition to the family's total wealth?

Question 3: Look at the wages paid to the count's staff. Who was paid the most? The least? Why?

Question 4: Look at the theater expenses for 1788. How many coachmen could the count have hired for a year with that amount of money?

Question 5: What event occurred in 1789 that probably resulted in significant changes in these figures for many years?

Table 18.5: Variations within the Russian Aristocracy in 1774 (p. 457)

This table breaks the Russian aristocracy into four categories, and then gives the approximate number of serfs owned by a member of each class. It also gives the percentage of the total aristocracy for the two poorest classes, with the top two classes having a combined total of 16 percent.

Question 1: Look at the column "serfs owned." What does this indicate about the status and degree of freedom of serfs in Russia in 1774?

Question 2: Why would there be a relationship between number of serfs owned and level of economic wealth?

Question 3: Which category is the most numerous? What conclusions can you draw from that fact?

Table 18.6: The Great Cities of Europe in 1700 (p. 462)

This table lists all cities in Europe that had a population of 70,000 or greater in the year 1700.

Question 1: Only one German city made the list, Hamburg at the bottom. Why do you think this is so?

Question 2: Excluding Constantinople, what were the two largest cities in 1700? How important are these cities in today's Europe?

Question 3: Which country has the most cities on the list? Does this change if you consider all the Italian states as one country?

Table 18.7: Manufacturing in Eighteenth-Century England (p. 464)

This table lists 11 categories of manufacturing in 1770 England, along with their percentage of total manufacturing output.

Question 1: The production of which product accounted for the highest percentage of total manufacturing output?

Question 2: What reasons can you give for the importance of textile manufacturing?

Question 3: Which material was responsible for the greatest percentage of textile manufacture? Why do you think this is so? Do you think it was the most desirable fabric for clothing? Why or why not?

Table 18.8: Estimated Slave Population of European Colonies in the Americas, 1770 (p. 471)

This table presents data on slavery in all the European colonies in the Americas. The first column lists the total estimated population in a country's American colonies. The second column lists the estimated slave population in those colonies, and the third column gives the ratio of the second column to the first, expressed as a percentage.

Question 1: How many European countries had colonies with slaves in the Americas?

Question 2: List the top two countries in terms of slave population in the colonies. Why do you think the second-ranking country was able to accommodate so many slaves in its colony?

Question 3: Which region had the greatest proportion of slaves to total population? How can you explain this?

ART INTERPRETATION

Illustration 18.3: Aristocratic Life (p. 454)

This painting was created by Jean-Honoré Fragonard. *Happy Accidents of the Swing* was commissioned by Baron de Saint-Julien in 1767, with his mistress the model for the lady in motion. At the baron's request, the person seen pushing the lady in the lower right is depicted as a bishop. The baron himself is at lower left.

Questions to ponder:

1. What do you think the "happy accident" is?

2. In what ways does this painting perpetuate the popular conception of aristocratic life?

3. Look at the clothes the man and woman are wearing. Do they look comfortable? What if the temperature were 90 degrees with high humidity?

4. What aspects of the painting help demonstration the motion of the woman?

5. What aspects of the painting hint at love and romance? (Hint: Who's the little fellow on the left?)

CHAPTER 19
DAILY LIFE IN THE OLD REGIME

TABLE ANALYSIS

Table 19.1: European Population Density (p. 476)

This table presents the average number of people living on a square mile of land for several countries in both the year 1700 and in the 1990s. Note that the increase in density was not constant between the countries. For example, the population of France increased about three-fold during the nearly 300-year period, while that of Belgium increased eight-fold. Various factors could account for the differences among the countries, among them: which countries lost the greatest percentage of men in wars; which suffered the most from famine and disease; which had higher standards of living and were thus able to provide a healthier diet and living conditions for the bulk of the population; the net effect of immigration and emigration; what percentage of the land was actually inhabitable, i.e. not mountainous or swamp or water; did the size of the country increase or decrease.

Question 1: Which country has experienced the greatest percentage population growth since 1700? Which country the least?

Question 2: Would the Europe of 1700 have been capable of supporting the population of modern-day Europe? Why or why not?

Table 19.2: Average Speed of Mailing a Letter from Venice in 1700 (p. 478)

This table provides average times in days for a letter to be delivered to various destinations in Europe from Venice. Look at the source of the information—maps—which means that these times are estimates. Check a map of Europe to refresh your memory of the locations of the cities in the table. There is a general increase of delivery time with distance, although there is probably not a constant number of miles traveled per day for the mail.

Question 1: What geographic, political, and seasonal factors could effect delivery time?

Question 2: What type of transport do you think was used to get a letter to London? Do you think a ship would be faster, even though it would have to travel farther?

Table 19.3: The Causes of Death in the Eighteenth Century (p. 479)

This table presents the top five causes of death in 1740 Edinburgh and 1990s United States, along with the percentage of all deaths caused by each disease. Note that there is apparently no overlap between the top causes of the two places. But perhaps many of the "old age" deaths of Edinburgh can be attributed to cancer and heart disease, illnesses that strike older people more than the young. Also note that neither set of five percentages adds up to 100 percent: it's 73.8 percent for Edinburgh and 71.0 percent for the United States, which means other causes of death were/are significant.

Question 1: What were likely causes of death to fill out the remaining 26 percent of deaths in the Edinburgh of 1740?

Question 2: What are the fundamental agents of death in 1740 Edinburgh (besides old age)? Compare these agents with the fundamental reasons for the development of heart disease, stroke, cancer, and pulmonary conditions in contemporary America.

Table 19.4: Grain Consumption in the Eighteenth Century (p. 486)

This table gives the average number of pounds of grain each person consumed per day for the given country and time period. Note the wide fluctuation in consumption, with Burgundians consuming 4.4 times as much as residents of Holland. Note also that the dates of measurement span nearly 100 years, meaning some of the comparisons are not exact.

Question 1: Which of the regions covered was likely the most prosperous, and why?

Question 2: What did a high level of grain consumption mean for the health of such consumers?

Table 19.5: Food in the Budget of a Berlin Worker's Family, c. 1800 (p. 486)

This table lays out the percentage of the total income spent on various food and nonfood items for a the family of a Berlin worker in 1800. Note the total percentage spent on bread, 45 percent, and then refer back to Table 19.4 for data on bread consumption. It is easy to understand why the lower classes were so concerned about the price of bread, and why they would occasionally riot when the price increased. Compara-tively little, 14 percent of total income, was spent on housing, a sub-stantial contrast with the cost of housing in the modern industrial soci-eties of today's Europe.

Question 1: What percentage of the Berlin family's total food expenditure was spent on bread? What does the indicate about the health of the family's diet? (Refer to Table 19.4)

Question 2: Compare the Berlin family's budget for food and non-food items with you own budget. Where are the main differences? What does this indicate about the standard of living of the average working family in 1800 Berlin?

Table 19.6: The Diet in an Amsterdam Prison, 1781 (p. 489)

This table presents the food given to Dutch prisoners (those who completed their work) over the course of a week. Quantities are given for some foods, but not all.

Question 1: What major food group is substantially underrepresented in the diet? How do you think this affected the health of the pri-soners?

Question 2: What other factors would affect the health of prisoners?

Table 19.7: A Comparison of Life Cycles (p. 492)

This table lists important demographic data for Sweden in the period 1778-1782 and the United States in 1990. For every birth and death characteristic, the data shows that present-day Americans were more likely to survive birth and live to an old age. Life expectancy at birth is the most telling statistic: Less than half of Swedes lived to see their fortieth birthday. Also note the infant mortality rate for Sweden is 23 times that of the present-day United States.

Question 1: How do you think low life-expectancy affected the mind-set and outlook of eighteenth century Swedes (and their contemporaries throughout Europe)? If you knew there was a 50-50 chance you'd be dead by age 45, what would you do differently in your life?

Question 2: Note the age distribution of the population of Sweden. How do you think having a greater percentage of the population in the 15-64 age group would affect economic production in eighteenth century Sweden, or any country at any time?

Table 19.8: Infant Mortality in the Eighteenth Century (p. 493)

This table gives the percentage of infants born alive that die before their first birthday for six different countries/regions. Data for the United States covers 1995 only; for the other five, data is given for three different time periods.

Question 1: What was the general trend in infant mortality over time? What factors do you think could account for the decrease?

Question 2: The data for the German states shows an increase in infant mortality. How can you account for this? Is it possible the data itself is inaccurate, or were conditions in the German states substantially different than in the other countries?

Table 19.9: Famine and Abandoned Children in France, 1692-1710 (p. 494)

This table gives the total number of abandoned children at two of France's major cities, Paris and Lyon.

Question 1: Does the data give any indication as to which of the two cities has the larger population? What assumptions are you making if you say that one is larger than the other?

Question 2: Compare the ratio of Lyon abandonments to Paris abandonments for each year. Are there substantial changes in the ratios? Could severity of famine be different in the two regions, or could there be other factors that account for any differences?

Table 19.10 Premarital Conception and Illegitimate Birth in the Old Regime (p. 502)

This table gives data on the percentage of premarital conceptions and percentage of illegitimate births for England, France, the German states, and Spain for three time-periods ending in 1820, along with the same data for the United States in the twentieth century.

Question 1: How do you account for the differences in the percentage of premarital conceptions and the percentages of illegitimate births for the same country in the same time period?

Question 2: What was the general trend in the two statistics over time? How can you explain it?

ART INTERPRETATION

Illustration 19.1: Coach Travel (p. 476)

Questions to ponder:

1. The sign on the hotel mentions "chevaliers," the French word for knights. What do you thinks this says about advertising in this time period?

2. None of the buildings rise above three or four stories. Why do you think this is so?

3. What is the condition of the streets in the town? Look at the couple walking in the street. Do you think they're looking at the majestic Pyrenees, enthralled by the grandeur of nature and their love for each other, or do you think they're looking in front of their feet for evidence of the prior passage of horses?

4. Given the condition of town streets, speculate on the condition of the roads that connected the towns. How pleasant do you think a 250-mile journey by coach would be on such roads? Do you think those coaches had some sort of shock absorbers?

5. So there's a broken wheel. What could have broken it? Does fixing it look more involved than changing a tire on a modern automobile?

CHAPTER TWENTY
THE POLITICAL EVOLUTION OF THE OLD REGIME, 1715-1789

TABLE ANALYSIS

Table 20.1 British War Finances, 1702-1783 (p. 515)

This table presents data on the amount of money the British government spent on four eighteenth-century wars. The first column presents the total expenditure for the war, the second government income for the war duration, the third the difference between the two, which is the amount the government had to borrow. The fourth column gives the percentage of the amount borrowed to the total amount spent. These wars were very expensive and resulted in a substantial drain on resources for Britain.

Question 1: Which war was the most expensive? In what ways could you argue that that war began because of Britain's previous war debt? What would Britain have needed to do in order to not have fought this war?

Question 2: From the data in the table, can you see any discernible relationship between duration of a war and the amount of money spent on it? Is the result counterintuitive? What factors can affect the cost of war? What factors can affect the comparison of the costs of wars fought at different time periods?

Question 3: Britain definitely paid a high price in monetary terms to fight these wars. What did it gain?

Table 20.2: Land Ownership in Ireland, 1603-1778 (p. 517)

This table presents the change in ownership in land in Ireland from the year 1603 through 1778. For each of five years during this period, the table gives the percentage of land owned by Catholics and the percentage of land owned by Protestants. As the length of the English occupation/colonization grew, the Catholic percentage decreased as the Protestant percentage increased.

Question 1: Where do you think most of the ten percent of the land owned by Protestants in 1603 was located? What is your reasoning for your answer?

Question 2: Were there significant numbers of non-Christian landowners in Ireland during this time period?

Question 3: There were significant numbers of Catholics in England during this time period. Do you think the government encouraged them to immigrate to Ireland? Why or why not?

Table 20.3: The Cost of Royal Extravagance, 1760 (p. 520)

This table lists the cost in livres of a jeweled writing desk built for the royal family by a Parisian jeweler in 1760.

Question 1: Which expenses are the most extravagant?

Question 2: Look at Table 18.4 and determine how many maids could have been employed for one year for 77,158 livres.

Question 3: Look at Table 18.4 and determine how many coachmen could have been employed for one year for 77,158 livres.

Table 20.4: French National Budget, 1774 (p. 520)

This table presents a simplified budget for France for the year 1774. There are five broad categories: army, which represents military spending; service on debt, which is the amount of money paid to the holders of government debts; royal court, the money spent to maintain the life-style of the king and all those officially part of the court; royal pensions, money paid by the government to various people, often aristocracy, for services rendered or as a payoff for political support; the last category includes all the other expenses of government.

Question 1: What would your financial situation be if you had to pay 30 percent of your income in credit card debt?

Question 2: What was the most costly expenditure? If there were no war, and government leaders knew there would never be war again, how would that have affected the national budget of France in 1774?

Question 3: What could have been some of the causes of the expenses in the "all other" category?

Chart 20.1: The Recession in French Agriculture, 1774-86 (p. 522)

This chart traces the profits and losses of lease-hold farmers in France from 1774 to 1786. These farmers did well during the first six years, but poorly thereafter.

Question 1: How could this decline in agricultural profits affect the political support of the French king?

Question 2: How many years resulted in losses, and how many in profits?

Question 3: What is a good estimate of the net average profit of French lease-hold farmers for this period?

ART INTERPRETATION

Illustration 20.7: Two Views of Enlightened Despotism in Austria (p. 525)

Questions to ponder:

1. How do the illustrations show the different ways in which the two Habsburg monarchs portrayed themselves?

2. In what ways does the painting of Joseph II demonstrate the "enlightened" side of his reign?

3. How does the painting of Maria Theresa portray her and her family? What messages would she most likely have wanted this painting to send to her subjects?

CHAPTER 21
THE CULTURE OF OLD REGIME EUROPE

TABLE ANALYSIS

Table 21.1: Ecclesiastical Populations in Catholic Europe (p. 549)

This table presents data regarding total population and the number of priests and persons in orders from three different areas of Catholic Europe in the eighteenth century. For the first two, the date of determination is given, followed by the total population, the number of priests, the percentage of priests in the total population, the number of people in orders, the percentage of the total population in orders, the total number of people in the church (the sum of those in priesthood and orders), followed by the percentage of all church people in the total population. The number of priests is missing for Vallodalid.

Question 1: How many priests would Vallodalid need to have in order to have 7.5 percent of its population in ecclesiastic activities?

Question 2: How can you explain the willingness of these communities or regions to support such large ecclesiastical communities?

Question 3: What evidence points to the idea that there were different levels of support for the Catholic Church in different regions of Europe?

ART INTERPRETATION

Illustration 21.6: The Salon of Madame Geoffrin (p. 545)

Questions to ponder:

1. What is the approximate ratio of men to women in the illustration? Does it seem to you that women were equals in these salons, or did they have more of a facilitating role?

2. Did the artist do a good job of portraying these people as looking intelligent? Can you imagine yourself sitting there, listening to the conversation, perhaps interjecting a witty or pithy comment?

3. What similarities do you see in the clothing style of the people in the salon? Hair style?

CHAPTER TWENTY-TWO
THE FRENCH REVOLUTION AND NAPOLEON, 1789-1815

TABLE ANALYSIS

Table 22.1: The Social Composition of Revolutionary Groups (p. 575)

This table presents data on the composition of six groups of people: people arrested at the Bastille in 1789; emigrés from 1789 to 1799; deputies of the convention, 1792-95; members of Jacobin clubs, 1793-95; victims of the terror, 1793-94; and Vendéen counterrevolutionaries, 1793. It presents much data on which members of which classes and occupations were involved in the various aspects of the French Revolution and its aftermath.

Part Four

Question 1: As a percentage of the total number in France in 1789, which class was probably the most highly represented of all the emigrés?

Question 2: Look at the composition of the convention deputies. Which had the most representatives? Are lawyers still active in politics in western countries?

Question 3: Look at the data on victims of the terror of 1793-94. Can you draw any strong conclusions about a definite class bias to the terror? Why or why not?

Table 22.2: The Reign of Terror, 1793-94 (p. 590)

This table presents data in four categories of activities related to the Reign of Terror: executions by the Paris Revolutionary Tribunal; total executions in France; crimes leading to capital sentences; and sentences of the Marseilles Tribunal in 1794. The first two categories are delineated by class, the third by type of crime, the fourth by sentence of the tribunal.

Question 1: Compare the data on executions by the Paris Revolutionary Tribunal with the data on total executions in France. What is the greatest class disparity between the two? The least?

Question 2: Which class most likely had the highest proportion of its members executed? Which class most likely had the lowest proportion?

Question 3: What was the most common crime leading to a capital sentence? Do you think this is still a capital crime in most of Europe today? What about Eastern Europe in the 1970s?

Question 4: What were the first and second most likely decisions of the Marseilles Tribunal in 1794? How does this accord with most criminal cases in today's Europe?

Table 22.3: The Military Campaigns of Napoleon, 1796-1815 (p. 594)

This table presents data on eight military campaigns conducted by Napoleon between 1796 and 1815. For each decisive battle in the campaign, the table provides the states at war (France is always one), the date, the size of each state's army, the size-advantage ratio for the larger army, the losses of each side in the battle, the percentage of army lost for each side, and, for most campaigns, the name of the resulting peace treaty. Overall, the data provides a wealth of information for analyzing the battles and outcomes.

Question 1: Were there any battles in which the side with the larger number of troops sustained the highest percentage of losses? What conclusions can you draw from your answer?

Question 2: Examine the data for the battles won and lost by France. What conclusions can you make about the importance of army size?

Question 3: What was the largest number of troops in a single battle for a side? Who won that battle and why was it so important?

Question 4: In what battle was the percentage of army lost for the two sides the greatest?

ART INTERPRETATION

Illustration 22.9: The Napoleonic Wars (p. 598)

Questions to ponder:

1. How is Napoleon portrayed in the two paintings? Which portrays him in a more favorable way?

2. In what ways can David's "Napoleon Crossing the Alps" be considered propaganda?

3. How does the use of light and color affect the overall impressions of the two paintings?

PART FIVE: EUROPE IN THE AGE OF INDUSTRIALIZATION, 1815-1914

CHAPTER TWENTY-THREE
INDUSTRIALIZATION AND THE SOCIAL AND ECONOMIC STRUCTURE OF EUROPE

TABLE ANALYSIS

Table 23.1: The European Population Explosion, 1700-1900 (p. 607)

This table gives population data for most of Europe for three different years: 1700, 1800, and 1900. It also gives the growth in percent for two time periods: 1700-1800 and 1800-1900. The overall trend is substantial growth in both centuries, especially the nineteenth. Some of the data is skewed due to the shifting of borders during the 200-year span.

Question 1: What factors could account for the higher rates of population growth in the nineteenth century as compared to the eighteenth century?

Question 2: Which country/region/empire experienced the greatest growth in the eighteenth century? The nineteenth century?

Question 3: Which country/ region/empire had the largest population in 1700? 1800? 1900?

Question 4: What are all the possible factors that could have affected population size in England and France in the eighteenth century?

Chart 23.1 The Vital Revolution: Birth and Death Rates in Britain, 1710-1820 (p. 609)

This chart traces the change in birth and death rates in Britain between 1710 and 1820.

Question 1: What was the overall trend in birth rates?

Question 2: What was the overall trend in death rates?

Table 23.2: The Growth of British Cities, 1801-51 (p. 610)

This table chronicles the growth of six British cities over a fifty-period, with data provided from a decennial census for 1801, 1811, 1821, 1831, 1841, and 1851.

Question 1: Which city had the greatest percentage growth between 1801 and 1851? Which had the least? What factors could account for different cities having different growth rates?

Question 2: What was the average increase in percentage growth between 1801 and 1851?

Question 3: What clue in the data lets you know that these numbers are not exact counts?

Table 23.3: The Major Cities of Europe, 1800-1900 (p. 610)

This table gives data on the population and ranking of the largest cities in Europe in 1800, 1850, and 1900.

Question 1: What was the percentage population increase for London between 1800 and 1850? How does this compare with the answers to Questions 1 and 2 for Table 23.2?

Question 2: Britain had seven cities on the 1850 list, but only three on the 1900 list. How can you account for this?

Question 3: Which city moved the farthest up the rankings between 1800 and 1900?

Question 4: For the top five cities in 1800, which experienced the largest percentage increase in population by 1900?

Question 5: Compare the data here with that in Table 18.6 on page 462. What conclusions can you draw from the comparison?

Table 23.4: European Coal Production, 1820-40 (p. 614)

This table gives the number of millions of tons of coal produced by each country for the years 1820, 1830, and 1840.

Question 1: Which country produced the most coal in all three years?

Question 2: Which country experienced the greatest increase in coal production between 1820 and 1840?

Question 3: Calculate Britain's share of total coal production of the total produced by all five countries for each year. Are there any conclusions you can draw from your calculations?

Table 23.5: The Beginning of the Railroad Age in Europe, 1825-50 (p. 619)

This table lists the number of kilometers of railway lines available for use in the major countries and regions of Europe for the years 1825, 1830, 1835, 1840, 1845, and 1850. The data is probably fairly accurate since it is relatively easy to calculate the length of rail lines, and a number of them still exist. Also, there are probably numerous written references to the railways.

Question 1: Which country or region had by far the greatest length of railways for all years listed? What does this say about the country's economic development?

Question 2: Which country or region had the second greatest number of kilometers of railway in 1850? What did this portend for industrialization over the next 50 to 60 years?

Question 3: In 1850 Russia had only 501 kilometers of railway, whereas France had 2,915 kilometers. What does this indicate?

Table 23.6: Employment in British Cotton Factories, by Gender, 1835 (p. 623)

This table presents data on the number of men and women employed in cotton factories in four regions of Britain in 1835: England, Ireland, Scotland, and Wales. The data demonstrates that women made up the majority of the workforce in these factories.

Question 1: Can you think of any reasons why women made up the smallest percentage of the cotton factory workforce in England?

Question 2: Where were the highest number of cotton-factory workers employed?

Table 23.7: The Labor Force in York, England, 1851 (p. 625)

This table lists eight categories of employment. For each category, the table gives the percentage of men engaged in that occupation (the number of men working in that category divided by the total number of men in the workforce) and the corresponding statistic for women. The table allows us to see which occupations men and women tended to choose, or were directed into.

Question 1: In what occupations were women most highly represented? How can you explain this?

Question 2: In what occupations were women most sparsely represented? How can you explain this?

Question 3: What was the ratio of men to women in the workforce?

Table 23.8: Death of Children Mineworkers in Britain in 1838 (p. 626)

This table presents data on the various causes of death for children working in mines. The data is broken down by age group of children: under 13, 13-18, and 18-21. Total deaths are given for each age group, and for each cause of death.

Question 1: What were the three most common causes of death?

Question 2: Which age group suffered the greatest number of deaths? The least number of deaths?

Question 3: Look at the total deaths by age category. Can you draw a conclusion as to which age group probably made up the greatest percentage of all employees under the age of 22? Upon what assumptions are you basing your conclusion?

Table 23.9: Child Labor in the French Textile Industry, 1845 (p. 626)

This table groups data into four columns: industry (type of textile manufactured or used); number of children employed in that industry; the ratio of children employed in that industry to the total number employed in that industry, expressed as a percent; and the percentage of all child labor employed in that industry. The rows give the data for the various textile industries.

Question 1: In which industry were children the greatest percentage of the workforce?

Question 2: Which industry employed the greatest number of children?

Question 3: In what other sectors of the economy could the remaining 27.6 percent of the child labor force have been employed?

Table 23.10: The Take-Off of Heavy Industry in Europe, 1851-69 (p. 632)

This table lists data on the production of iron and coal in Austria, Britain, France, and the German states (Zollverein) for 1851, 1860, and 1869. It also gives the percentage increase in the two raw materials for each country between 1851 and 1869.

Question 1: Which country or country group experienced the greatest growth in the production of coal and iron? Which experienced the least growth?

Question 2: Who was the leader in coal and iron production for all three years? What conclusions can your draw from this about the level of industrialization of that country compared with the others?

Question 3: If production of coal and iron were the main sources of international power, which country or country grouping had the greatest percentage increase in power between 1851 and 1869? Did that make it the most powerful country or country grouping? Why or why not?

Table 23.11: European Railroad Expansion, 1850-70 (p. 632)

This table lists the number of kilometers of railroad track in use for most major European countries for the years 1850, 1860, and 1870. Compare it with the data in Table 23.5 on page 619.

Question 1: Which country had the greatest length of railroad track in all three measurement years? What does this indicate about the level of industrialization and economic development in that country at that time?

Question 2: What piece of demographic data for each country would allow a better comparison of degree of use of railroads?

Question 3: Which country had the greatest percentage increase in length of track between 1850 and 1870? Do you think this could also be a power indicator? (See Table 23.10 questions above)

Question 4: Given the size of the country and the population, what was the long-term significance for Russia being so relatively far behind the other major powers in total rail-line length?

ART INTERPRETATION

Illustration 23.6: The Nineteenth-Century Urban World (p. 620)

Questions to ponder:

1. Which town or city do you think would most likely have the highest per-capita crime rate? Upon what assumptions are you basing your conclusion?

2. Which of the three towns or cities would you rather have lived in 1850? Why?

3. Which picture illustrates a scene closest to medieval times? Why?

CHAPTER TWENTY-FOUR
DAILY LIFE IN THE NINETEENTH CENTURY

TABLE ANALYSIS

Table 24.1: Life Expectancy in the Nineteenth Century (p. 638)

This table gives data on the life expectancy at birth for males and females for different years and ranges of years for several European countries and the United States. There are three major times: a year or range of years in the nineteenth century, a year or range near the beginning of the twentieth century, and the year 1989.

Question 1: What was the overall trend in the data?

Question 2: What reasons explain the trend noticed in Question 1?

Question 3: On average, women live longer than men, then and now. How can you explain this fact?

Question 4: For each of the three main time periods, determine which country had the highest male life expectancy, which country had the highest female life expectancy, which country had the lowest male life expectancy, and which country had the lowest female life expectancy.

Table 24.2: The Death Rate in England from Infectious Diseases, 1848-1901 (p. 640)

This table lists the number of deaths per million population in England in 1848 and 1901 for a variety of diseases and causes. There are five main categories of death: airborne diseases, water- and food-borne dis-eases, sexually transmitted diseases, other diseases attributable to microorganisms, and "other."

Question 1: Which diseases resulted in more deaths per million in 1901 than in 1848? How can you account for this? Think of all possible factors: diet, environment, social changes, economic changes, etc. Don't neglect the possibility of misdiagnosis, especially in 1848.

Question 2: For each year, which category of disease resulted in the greatest number of deaths?

Question 3: Which diseases do you think would most likely be more prevalent in urban areas?

Question 4: Which causes of death would probably be the hardest to diagnose? Why?

Table 24.3: The Hamburg Cholera Epidemic of 1892 (p. 643)

This table presents data that shows the differential effects of cholera on the various economic classes in Hamburg in 1892. There are eight income categories, with three columns giving the number of people in each category, the percentage of each category that contracted cholera, and the percentage in each category that died of cholera.

Question 1: What is the general relationship between income and likelihood of contracting cholera? What factors led to this?

Question 2: For each income category calculate the ratio of the percentage who died to the percentage who caught the disease. In which income category was a person who caught cholera most likely to die of the disease? How can you explain the result?

Question 3: Do you think rural areas around Hamburg had higher or lower overall death rates from cholera in 1892? Why?

Table 24.4: The Average Height of European Military Recruits (p. 647)

This table presents data on the average height of soldiers for several European countries. The first column lists the country. The second column lists the average height in feet and inches along with the date determined. The third column lists average height in feet and inches in 1900. Note the different dates of determination for the second column, and that no data was available for France and Norway.

Question 1: What was the overall average height increase, in inches, in 1900 as compared to the earlier determination?

Question 2: What factors could account for the increase in average height?

Question 3: Do you think the average height of military recruits is higher now than in 1900? Why or why not?

Table 24.5: The Average Daily Diet at Antwerp in the 1850s (p. 647)

This table gives extensive data on the average daily diet of a resident of Antwerp in the 1850s. The first column lists the various food sources in the diet. The second column gives the average consumption per person, per day, in either grams or liters. The third column lists the total num-ber of calories from each source per day. The fourth column lists the percentage of total categories from that source per day.

Question 1: Which food source accounted for the greatest weight of food? How easy do you think it was to produce and store this food source?

Question 2: What was the main source of carbohydrates?

Question 3: Which food had the highest number of calories per gram?

Question 4: Look at the data for beer consumption. Do you think every person drank that amount of beer per day? What does this say about the "average" diet in Antwerp?

Question 5: What main food group is missing from this table? How would a lack of this food group affect the health of Antwerp residents?

Table 24.6: Opium Use in England, 1827-77 (p. 652)

This table lists data on English opium imports, total home consumption (consumed in Britain, in tons), and home consumption (per 1000 population, in pounds) for 1827, 1837, 1847, 1857, 1867, and 1877. Consumption data was not available for the latter two years.

Question 1: In what year was the total amount of opium imports highest?

Question 2: What was the general trend in opium use between 1827 and 1857?

Question 3: Do you think the missing values for 1867 and 1877 were higher or lower than the 1857 values? How did you reach your conclusion?

Chart 24.1: The Declining Birth Rate in France, Britain, and Germany, 1810-1910 (p. 653)

This chart traces changes in the birth rate in France, Britain, and Germany between 1810 and 1910. The y-axis gives the number of births per 10,000 population per year. The x-axis gives the years.

Question 1: Which country had the highest birth rate for this hundred-year period?

Question 2: What factors could account for relatively abrupt increases and decreases?

Question 3: What factors could help explain why three countries in the same region of the world would have substantially different birth rates?

Table 24.7: The Declining Birthrate in Europe, 1840-1914 (p. 656)

This table well demonstrates the declining birthrate in Europe for the time period 1840-1910. The birth rate is given as births per 1000 population and is provided at ten-year intervals from 1840 to 1910, and then for 1914. The percentage decline for each country is also given for the time period, though this period is shorter for the last three countries due to a lack of data. The percentage decline is computed by subtracting the 1914 value from the 1840 value, and then dividing that number by the 1840 value.

Question 1: What was the average percentage decline for the first four countries between 1840 and 1914?

Question 2: Which country had the highest birthrate in 1860?

Question 3: How do you think this data was obtained? What are some possible reasons why it was not gathered in Russia and Spain prior to 1860?

Table 24.8: Abandoned Children in St. Petersburg, 1830-45 (p. 657)

This table presents data on the number and percentages of abandoned children in St. Petersburg, Russia for the years 1830, 1835, 1840, and 1845.

Question 1: What general conclusions can you draw about how serious child abandonment was in St. Petersburg at this time?

Question 2: What factors make it difficult to have a lot of confidence in the numbers?

Table 24.9: The Rise of Universal Education in Europe, 1849-1914 (p. 658)

This table illustrates the substantial increase in people obtaining both primary and university-level education in Europe from the middle of the nineteenth century through the early years of the twentieth century. For most European countries, the number of pupils is given, with the year of determination in parentheses. Note that the year of determination varies from country to country.

Question 1: Which country had the greatest percentage increase in university students? Calculate this by dividing the difference in the number of students by the number of years between determinations, and then multiplying by 100 to get a percentage.

Question 2: Which country had the largest number of university students in 1910, as near as you can tell?

Question 3: What are the economic, political, and social implications of a more-educated populace?

Table 24.10: The Decline of Illiteracy in Europe, 1800-1910 (p. 661)

This table uses a crude but useful method of measuring illiteracy: signing a wedding certificate with an "X." The data is incomplete, and is presented for England, France, Italy, Prussia, and Germany, for various years beginning with 1800 and ending in 1910.

Question 1: As near as you can tell, which country experienced the most substantial decline in illiteracy?

Question 2: Which country do you think had the most literate population (at least of newlyweds) in 1840? How did you make your determination?

Question 3: Why would it not be wise to make sweeping conclusions about literacy in these countries based solely on this data?

Table 24.11: Marriage Patterns in Nineteenth-Century Europe (p. 662)

This table gives data on marriage in three places in nineteenth-century Europe. The mean age of marriage in Belgium in the year 1800 is broken down by occupation and gender. The mean age of marriage in Württemburg from 1880 to 1914 is also broken down by occupation and gender. Teenage marriage in a Russian province is given for three different years for each teen age as a percentage of all marrying females or males.

Question 1: In which of the three cases studied did people marry at the youngest age? How did you make your determination?

Question 2: What was the age trend in teenage marriage in the Russian province between 1782 and 1868?

Question 3: Looking at all three examples, can you make any generalizations about the age of men at marriage relative to that of women at the age of marriage? Does this accord with what you may have learned in other courses about modern society, or your general observations of modern society?

Table 24.12: Family Size in Württemburg in the 1850s and 1860s (p. 663)

This table gives the percentage of families with the given number of children (see column headings) for three types of occupations of the fathers of the families: agriculture, metal industry, textile industry.

Question 1: What should be the approximate sum of each of the three rows?

Question 2: Which occupation was most likely to have no children?

Question 3: Which occupation was most likely to have seven or more children?

ART INTERPRETATION

Illustration 24.11: Venereal Disease (p. 667)
Questions to ponder:

1. How effective do you think the illustration is at making people realize the consequences of promiscuous sexual activity? If the clothing were changed, would it be an effective safer-sex poster for today?

2. Based on the clothing and setting, what class do you think is represented in the illustration?

3. Who is the little guy in the upper right? What message does his body language and facial expression convey?

CHAPTER TWENTY-FIVE
THE DEFENSE OF THE OLD REGIME, 1815-48

TABLE ANALYSIS

Table 25.1: The British Aristocracy in the Early Nineteenth Century (p. 695)

This table lists and numbers two main categories of early nineteenth-century British aristocracy. The nobility includes temporal lords with various aristocratic titles, and also spiritual lords—archbishops and bishops. The lesser nobility are broken into four categories, along with the number of families in each category.

Question 1: Do you think the nobility or the lesser nobility had the greatest numbers?

Question 2: Why do you think spiritual lords were included in the nobility? What does this say about the place of the Anglican Church in British society?

ART INTERPRETATION

Illustration 25.1: The Congress of Vienna (p. 673)

Questions to ponder:

1. How can you tell who the most important people in the room are?

2. Does the decor and nature of the room match the grandeur of the scope of the international politics taking place in it?

3. How does the fashion of high-ranking men of the time differ with modern men's fashion in western societies?

CHAPTER TWENTY-SIX
EUROPE IN AN AGE OF NATIONALISM

TABLE ANALYSIS

Table 26.1: Casualties in the Crimean War, 1853-56 (p. 721)

This table provides much data on Crimean War participants, including army size, the number and percent killed by wounds, the number and percent killed by disease, the total number and percent of losses (deaths), the number and percent of wounded, and the number and percent of total casualties (those killed or wounded in battle, not count-ing disease. Some of the data is missing for some of the participants.

Question 1: Which was the greater cause of death: wounds or disease? How do you think that compares with late-twentieth century wars?

Question 2: Which country had the greatest number of total losses? The least?

Question 3: Which country had the greatest percentage of its troops killed?

Question 4: Which side had the larger army?

Table 26.2: Serfs and Peasants in Imperial Russia, 1858 (p. 723)

This table uses data from the 1858 census in Russia to obtain the numbers and working status of serfs and peasants.

Question 1: Where were most peasants located? What does this indicate?

Question 2: Where were most serfs located?

Question 3: Which group was larger, serfs or peasants?

Table 26.3: The Growth of European Standing Armies, 1830-60 (p. 729)

This table gives the size of the army in 1830 and 1860 for Austria, France, Prussia, and Russia, four of the five major European powers of the time. It also gives the percentage growth of each army between the two dates.

Question 1: Which country's army experienced the greatest percentage growth between 1830 and 1860? Which had the smallest percentage growth?

Question 2: Which country had the largest army in 1830? Which had the smallest?

Question 3: Which country had the largest army in 1860? Which had the smallest?

ART INTERPRETATION

Illustration 26.7: Florence Nightengale and Modern Nursing (p. 722)

Questions to ponder:

1. How does this hospital differ from modern hospitals?

2. How does this hospital differ from most other war-time hospitals of the same time period?

3. Who is performing what jobs?

CHAPTER TWENTY-SEVEN
EUROPE IN THE BELL ÉPOQUE

TABLE ANALYSIS

Chart 27.1: Anglo-German Industrial Competition, 1880-1909
(p. 739)

This chart contains two parts. The top graph shows the increased consumption of coal and lignite in Britain and Germany. The combined total of these two energy sources runs along the y-axis in millions of tons. Years are along the x-axis. Similarly, the bottom graph traces consumption of pig iron in the same units over the same time period.

Question 1: At what year did German pig iron consumption equal that of Britain's? What is the margin of error of your estimate (how many years might you be off, due to the scale of the graph and difficulties in accurately determining the meeting point of the two lines)?

Question 2: Is there a certain year, or span of two to three years, in which the rate of German consumption of coal and lignite, and its consumption of pig iron, increased? What could have accounted for this?

Table 27.1: The Democratization of the British Electorate, 1831-86
(p. 746)

This table provides data on the number of eligible voters, and the number of those voters as a percentage of the total population, for three different regions—England and Wales, Scotland, Ireland—for six years during the time span between 1831 and 1886. The combined data for all three regions is given in the final column.

Question 1: How easy do you think it was to obtain the data for this table? What were the primary sources needed?

Question 2: Which region had the highest percentage of eligible voters relative to the total population? How can you explain this?

Question 3: Which region had the highest total number of eligible voters? How can you explain this?

Question 4: What was the overall trend in both the number of eligible voters and the ratio of those voters to the total population over time?

Question 5: How do you think these percentages compare with modern numbers?

Table 27.2: The Imperial Russian Budget for 1891 (p. 751)

This table presents dozens of monetary amounts grouped into two main categories: anticipated revenue and anticipated expenses. Modern countries make budgets similar to this one. On the revenue side are direct taxes: revenues that the government collects directly from citizens. Below that are the indirect taxes, such as taxes on tobacco and alcohol, that are collected by merchants and passed on to the government. Below that are moneys paid to the government by peasants, money from loans and investments, and a few miscellaneous categories, such as the rents of state lands. On the expenses side are the various departments of government, departments that are similar to those found in the European governments of today. In addition there is the money necessary to provide for the monarchy, and also the money needed to pay the principle and interest on money the government has borrowed.

Question 1: What was the largest source of indirect taxes? Do you think modern European governments also impose a tax on this substance?

Question 2: What is the largest single expense? What does this say about the perceived importance of the service for which the money was allocated for?

Question 3: What is the ratio of the annual total debt repayment to anticipated revenue? Do you think modern European countries tend to have a higher or lower ratio? Why?

Question 4: Is the budget balanced? (Do anticipated revenues equal anticipated expenditures?) What factors could lead to a budget deficit? A budget surplus?

Question 5: What are the major forms of direct and indirect taxes in the country where you live?

Table 27.3: European Steel Production, 1871-1911 (p. 757)

This table lists the output of steel, in tons, for ten European countries for the years 1871, 1891, and 1911.

Question 1: Why could steel production be considered a measure of a country's power?

Question 2: Compare the data in this table with that of Chart 27.1. What conclusions can you draw? Why?

Question 3: Which country produced the most steel in each year?

Question 4: Which country had the greatest percentage increase in steel production between 1871 and 1911? Between 1891 and 1911?

Table 27.4: The Average Workweek of the 1890s (p. 758)

This table lists 14 occupations along with the corresponding number of hours a practitioner of that profession worked in an average week in Britain and France.

Question 1: Can you draw a general conclusion as to whether the French worked more hours than the British, at least in these 14 occupations?

Question 2: What was the occupation that required the least number of hours of work per week in Britain? In France?

Question 3: What was the occupation that required the greatest number of hours of work per week in Britain? In France?

Table 27.5: The Growth of Union Membership in the Early Twentieth Century (p. 759)

This table provides numbers of the total union membership of nine European countries for five different years during the time period 1890 to 1913. Data is missing for several countries at different times.

Question 1: What are some possible explanations for why Russia only collected data in 1905? Why not before or after?

Question 2: As near as you can tell with the incomplete data, which country had the greatest number of union members in 1913?

Question 3: Which country had the greatest percentage increase in union membership between 1905 and 1913?

Table 27.6: Strikes in Europe, 1896-1910 (p. 759)

This table lists data for three time periods—1896-1900, 1901-1905, and 1906-1910—for four countries: Belgium, Britain, France, and Germany. For each country and time period it lists the average number of strikes per year and the total number of worker days lost.

Question 1: Which country or countries showed an increase in number of worker days lost per time period over time?

Question 2: Which country lost the greatest number of worker days in any of the three five-year periods?

Question 3: What is the more important statistic for determining the impact of strikes on a country's economic performance: average annual number of strikes or total number of worker days lost? Why?

Table 27.7: Socialist Deputies in European Parliaments, 1880-1914 (p. 761)

This table lists the number of socialist deputies in the parliaments of seven European countries as measured in five-year intervals beginning with 1880 and ending with 1914 (the only exception to the five-year interval pattern). It also shows the percentage of seats in the 1914 parliaments that were held by socialists.

Question 1: Which country was the first to elect socialists to parliament?

Question 2: Which country had the greatest percentage of socialists in parliament in 1914? Do you know post-World War II reputation of this country? Do you think the socialists ever came to power in this country?

Question 3: Why do you think the percentage of socialist deputies is listed for the year 1914 instead of 1915?

Question 4: Germany had a substantial number of socialists in its parliament from the mid-1880s on. How can you reconcile this with the fact that Germany was a monarchy with a very weak legislature?

ART INTERPRETATION

Illustration 27.10: Picasso and the Revolution against Representational Art (p. 766)

Spaniard Pablo Picasso (1881-1973) is generally considered the greatest artist of the twentieth century. At the beginning of the century he began his radical departure from all preceding art by shifting dramatically away from realist depictions of scenes, paving the way for modern art. *Demoiselles d'Avignon*, painted in 1907, demonstrates his early experimentation with cubism. He created over 20,000 works of art.

Questions to ponder:

1. How did this work differ from the typical depiction of nudes in art?

2. In what ways can this picture be considered flat? Is there much three-dimensional depth to it?

3. How do you think traditionalists in art viewed this painting when it was first created?

PART SIX: EUROPE IN THE AGE OF MASS SOCIETY, SINCE 1914

CHAPTER TWENTY-EIGHT
IMPERIALISM, WAR, AND REVOLUTION, 1881-1920

TABLE ANALYSIS

Table 28.1: The European Army Buildup, 1879-1913 (p. 789)

This table presents data on the size of the military, both in peacetime and fully mobilized for war, for the five major European powers for the years 1879 and 1913.

Question 1: Which country had the largest fully mobilized army in 1879? In 1913?

Question 2: Which country had the greatest percentage increase in fully mobilized army size between 1879 and 1913?

Question 3: Which country maintained the largest standing army as a proportion of the army size when fully mobilized for war?

Question 4: What did the large increase in army size portend for World War I?

Table 28.2: Life on the Home Front in World War I (p. 797)

This table contains two sets of data. The first gives data on inflation during wartime in France, Germany, Britain, and Italy by giving the percentage of prices of consumer goods for the given year as a percentage of the prices for those same goods in 1913. Numbers over 100 mean inflation occurred; the higher the number, the greater the inflation. The second set of data depicts the dire food shortages in Germany during the war. It lists nine food staples, along with the percentage of these staples Germans received compared to the 1913 diet for two periods toward the latter part of the war.

Question 1: Which country had experienced the greatest inflation by 1918? 1919?

Question 2: What could be the main causes of wartime inflation?

Question 3: What does the data on wartime rations indicate about the degree of famine in Germany toward the end of the war?

Table 28.3: Losses in World War I, 1914-18 (p. 800)

This table presents data on the losses of fifteen participants in World War I. It includes data on the number of combat deaths, the number of civilian deaths, and the total percentage of population killed in the war.

Question 1: Which country lost the greatest percentage of its population in the war?

Question 2: What were the top five countries in terms of total men mobilized?

Question 3: What were the top five countries in terms of total combat deaths?

Question 4: What was the average percentage of forces killed for the five major powers of Europe? What was the average percentage of forces wounded for those same five countries?

Table 28.4: The Cost of Basic Russian Consumer Goods, 1914-17 (p. 801)

This table presents the cost of seven commodities, including five food staples, in April 1914 and April 1917. Values are given in rubles, with 100 kopecks to the ruble. The data give a good indication of the high rate of inflation for this three-year period.

Question 1: Compute the percentage increase for each commodity. How do these percentages compare with the inflation rates for consumer goods found in Table 28.2?

Question 2: Who do you think the masses are most likely to blame for such large prices increases of the necessities of life? Could the inflation have contributed to the success of the Bolshevik Revolution?

ART INTERPRETATION

Illustration 28.8: The Rise of Antiwar Sentiment (p. 799)

Questions to ponder:

1. What did artist George Grosz hope to convey about the German military with this drawing?

2. Do you think most people would realize that this was an anti-war drawing? Why or why not?

3. Do you think most people would realize the point Grosz wanted to make about the role of big business and industry in the promulgation of the war?

CHAPTER TWENTY-NINE
EUROPE IN THE AGE OF DICTATORSHIP, 1919-39

TABLE ANALYSIS

Table 29.1: Industrial Recovery after World War I (p. 813)

This table provides data on outputs of crude steel and coal for 11 years between 1913 and 1928 for Belgium, France, and Germany. Numbers are given in thousands of metric tons. Note that there was not a smooth progression of increase (or decrease).

Question 1: What could account for the shift in German output in 1923 and 1924? Why were Belgium and France not affected?

Question 2: Calculate the ratio of France's output of crude steel to that of Germany's for each year. In what year is the ratio greatest? What year was it lowest? What is the overall trend in the data? What conclusions could you draw from the data?

Question 3: Why was 1919 marked by a decrease in production compared to 1913 for both materials for all three countries?

Table 29.2: Deficit Financing of World War I National Budgets, 1914-18 (p. 814)

This table lists the expenditures, income, and deficits for the period 1914-18 (in billions of 1913 U.S. dollars) for France, Germany, Great Britain, Russia, and the United States. It allows us to see not only the national income for these countries during this time period, but also to examine the size of each country's budget deficit.

Question 1: Which country had the highest deficit? Which had the lowest?

Question 2: What could be the impact of high budget deficits on government spending?

Table 29.3: The Decline of Infant Mortality in Europe, 1900-1940 (p. 817)

This table provides data on infant mortality, defined here as deaths of infants under one year of age that were born live, for Austria, Britain, France, Germany, Russia, and Sweden for the years 1900, 1910, 1920, 1930, and 1940. The overall trend was a substantial decline in infant mortality during the 40-year time span.

Question 1: Which country consistently had the lowest infant mortality rate?

Question 2: Which country had the highest infant mortality rate in 1900?

Question 3: What factors contributed to the lowering of infant mortality rates?

Table 29.4: Unemployment During the Great Depression, 1930-39 (p. 824)

This table presents the unemployment rate for the United States, Britain, Germany, the Netherlands, Norway, and Poland for every year between 1930 and 1939.

Question 1: What was the highest unemployment rate on the entire table? Which country had this rate?

Question 2: For each country, look for a three-year continuous span when unemployment rates tended to be highest. Compare these time periods between countries. Were they always the same? Does this mean the worst part of the Depression hit different countries at somewhat different times?

Question 3: Which country achieved the lowest unemployment rates? How did it accomplish this?

Table 29.5: Inflation and the Cost of Living in Italy, 1914-21 (p. 828)

This table traces the rising cost of living in Italy between 1914 and 1921. It gives the cost of living index for each year (using 1914 as a base of 100) and it gives the annual inflation rate for each year.

Question 1: In what year was the inflation rate the greatest? What could have accounted for this?

Question 2: How was the inflation rate calculated?

Question 3: Do you think the high rate of inflation helped or hindered Mussolini in his quest to seize power in Italy?

Table 29.6: Soviet Industrialization Under the Five Year Plan, 1928-32 (p. 837)

This table lists seven aspects of economic production. For each aspect it lists the 1928 total output, the 1932 target production of the Five Year Plan, and the actual 1932 total output.

Question 1: Did the Soviet Union meet the target goals?

Question 2: Calculate the percentage increase in each of the seven areas. Was the increase substantial? How do you think it compares with typical increases in those same categories for other European countries for a similar time span in the twentieth century?

Question 3: What factors account for the increased output during the Five Year Plan?

ART INTERPRETATION

Illustration 29.4: Dada (p. 818)

Questions to ponder:

1. How do you think the art world of the 1920s reacted to Duchamp's depiction of Mona Lisa with a mustache?

2. In what ways was the Dada movement similar to later rebellions against conventional values, such as the 1960s counterculture and the punk and slacker movements that followed?

CHAPTER THIRTY
EUROPE IN AN AGE OF TOTAL WAR: WORLD WAR II, 1939-45

TABLE ANALYSIS

Table 30.1: The Estimated Casualties of World War II (p. 859)

This table provides estimates of the number of people killed in combat, the number of people wounded, the number of civilians killed, and the total number killed for 16 allied countries and seven axis countries in World War II.

Question 1: Which country suffered the greatest number killed?

Question 2: What is the estimate range for the total number killed in the war for all the countries listed in the table?

Question 3: Why do you think Poland had so many civilians killed?

Question 4: What is the ratio range for the total number of USSR citizens killed to total number of United States citizens killed?

Question 5: How do the numbers of dead in World War II compare to the numbers for World War I? (See Table 28.3 on page 800)

ART INTERPRETATION

Illustration 30.1: The Nazi-Soviet Nonaggression Pact (p. 846)

Questions to ponder:

1. What is the irony depicted in the cartoon? How well does the artist portray it?

2. What is the significance of the man lying between Hitler and Stalin? What does he represent?

3. What is the significance of the guns present in the cartoon?

CHAPTER THIRTY-ONE
THE SOCIAL AND ECONOMIC STRUCTURE OF CONTEMPORARY EUROPE

TABLE ANALYSIS

Table 31.1: The Growth of European Population, 1700-1990 (p. 870)

This table provides population numbers for many of the major European countries. It includes estimates of the 1700 population and census data for the years 1900 and 1990, with all numbers in millions.

Question 1: Which country had the second-largest population in 1990?

Question 2: Which country had the greatest approximate growth between 1700 and 1990? What about between 1900 and 1990?

Question 3: Calculate the percentage increase per century for all Europe for the period 1700-1900 and for 1900-1990. Was there a significant difference? How can you explain the difference?

Table 31.2: The Growth of European Cities, 1900-91 (p. 872)

This table lists four types of data for the major cities of Europe: the 1991 world ranking, the 1991 population in millions, the 1900 population, and the 1991 population density per square mile.

Question 1: Which city had the largest population in 1991? Which had the highest population density?

Question 2: Which city experienced the greatest population growth between 1900 and 1991?

Question 3: None of the top ten largest cities in 1991 were in Europe. Where do you think they were?

Table 31.3: The Slow Urbanization of Eastern Europe (p. 872)

This table lists the percentage of urban population in 1970 and 1985 for nine Eastern European countries.

Question 1: Which country had the largest percentage of its population living in urban areas in 1985?

Question 2: Which country had the greatest percentage change in the percentage of urban population between the two years? Which had the least?

Question 3: What factors lead to increased urbanization?

Table 31.4: Commonwealth Immigration into Britain (p. 874)

This table presents data on the annual net immigration from the various British Commonwealth countries into Britain for four time periods between 1960 and 1972. Net immigration is the difference between the number immigrating into Britain and the number emigrating out of Britain. The data is broken into three geographic categories.

Question 1: What is the overall trend in net migration over the twelve-year span?

Question 2: Of the regions listed in the table, which accounted for the highest percentage of net immigration between 1960 and 1972?

Question 3: How could you explain the large discrepancy between the first half and second half of 1962?

Table 31.5: The Persistence of Agricultural Society (p. 875)

This table gives the percentages of the population employed in agriculture and industry for five major European countries around the turn of the twentieth century.

Question 1: Look at the sources and footnote for this table. Can you foresee any potential problems in combining data from more than one source?

Question 2: What is the main message of this table?

Question 3: Which country had the greatest percentage employed in agriculture? Which had the least? What conclusions can you draw about the level of economic development in these two countries?

Table 31.6: The Decline of Agricultural Employment (p. 875)

This table presents data on the percentage of the labor force engaged in agriculture for six different countries in three time periods: around 1910, around 1930, and around 1960.

Question 1: Which country (excluding Ireland) had the greatest decrease between the 1910 era and the 1961 era?

Question 2: How can you account for the substantial differences between Northern Ireland and the Republic of Ireland?

Question 3: What factors help account for the substantial decline in the percentage of labor force engaged in agriculture?

Table 31.7: The Growth of European Industrial Output, 1913-80 (p. 877)

This table gives data on the increased industrial output of various European countries during the twentieth century. All data is given relative to Britain in 1900, with that output being set at 100 for comparison purposes.

Question 1: Which three countries experienced the greatest percentage growth between 1953 and 1980? What does this say about Britain's declining status as a major power in the world?

Question 2: How do you think the authors of the sources measured "industrial output"?

Question 3: What type of data would you need in order to compare how well each country industrialized, given the number of people it contained? Look at Table 31.1 and use the 1990 estimates to calculate which country had the greatest industrial output per capita in 1980.

Table 31.8: The Socioeconomic Structure of Twentieth-Century Europe (p. 880)

This table lists the percentage of the population working in agriculture, industry, and the service sector for most European countries for the years 1910, 1930, 1950, 1960, and 1980. Check the footnotes for impor-tant caveats about the data.

Question 1: Compute the average percentages in the service sector for each year. What was the overall trend with time?

Question 2: Compute the average percentages in the agriculture sector for each year. What was the overall trend with time?

Question 3: Which sector changed the least, on average?

Table 31.9: Women in the European Labor Force, 1910-90 (p. 883)

This table presents the percentage of women in the total labor force for the years 1910, 1930, 1950, 1970, and 1990 for Britain, France, Germany, Italy, and Sweden.

Question 1: What was the general trend over time?

Question 2: Which country had the greatest percentage of women in the labor force in 1990? Which had the least? Do you think its possible to draw any conclusions about why there was such a difference between these two countries?

Question 3: Which twenty-year span saw the greatest percentage change? How can you account for this?

Table 31.10: The Twentieth-Century Decline in Death Rates (p. 884)

This table gives data on death rates, measured as the number of deaths per 1000 population per year, for ten countries at four different years spanning eight decades of the twentieth century.

Question 1: What is the overall trend in death rates? How can you account for it?

Question 2: Which country experienced the greatest percentage decline in death rates between 1910 and 1990?

Question 3: In your estimate, which year had the least amount of variation in death rates among the countries?

Table 31.11: The Twentieth-Century Decline in Infant Mortality (p. 885)

This table gives data on the number infants born alive that died before their first birthday for seven European countries and four non-European countries, all over a time span ranging from 1850 to 1990. Note that much of the data is not available for several countries for dates before 1990.

Question 1: What is the overall trend in infant mortality? Take a look at Table 19.8 on page 493. Does the data there fit the trend you see in the twentieth century?

Question 2: Which countries had the highest infant mortality rates in 1990? How can you account for this?

Question 3: Is there a substantial difference between western European and eastern European countries in the second half of the twentieth century? How can you account for the difference?

Question 4: What could account for the differences in infant mortality rates between whites and blacks in the United States?

Table 31.12: The Growth of Life Expectancy in Twentieth-Century Britain (p. 885)

This table gives the government estimate of the average age a person at the given age could expect to reach. Data is given for both males and females for ages 0, 1, and 10, and for the years 1901, 1931, 1961, 1991, and estimated 2001. All data is for Britain.

Question 1: In 1901 a male at birth had a life expectancy of 45.5 years, whereas a male at age 10 could expect to live to an age of 60.4. The corresponding numbers for 1991 were 73.2 and 73.9. How can you explain the nearly 15-year difference in 1901 with the .7 year difference in 1991?

Question 2: What factors could account for the fact that women in modern Britain (and many contemporary societies) outlive men by several years?

Question 3: Compare the data in this table with that of Table 24.1 on page 638. What conclusions can you draw?

Table 31.13: Divorce in Europe, 1910-90 (p. 886)

This table gives data on the number of divorces in 1910 and 1990, and divorces as a percentage of marriages in 1990, for six European countries. Note that data is unavailable for some countries and dates.

Question 1: What could account for the relatively low level of divorce in Italy?

Question 2: Which country had the greatest percentage of divorces as a percentage of marriages in 1990?

Question 3: What data would you need to get a more accurate comparison of divorce rates for the listed countries for 1910 and 1990?

Table 31.14: The Decline in European Birthrates, 1910-90 (p. 887)

This table presents the number of births per year per 1,000 population for nine European countries at four different times between 1910 and 1990.

Question 1: Which country had the largest decline in birth rates between 1910 and 1990? How can you account for this?

Question 2: Which year had some countries buck the trend of declining birthrates?

Table 31.15: Legal Abortions, 1967-90 (p. 889)

This table contains three separate sets of data. The topmost provides the numbers of legal abortions in England for married and unmarried women between the years 1967 and 1990. The middle gives rates of legal abortions per 1,000 population for the year 1989 for 12 countries. The bottom provides the percentage of pregnancies terminated by abortion for five countries in 1990.

Question 1: Can you conclude that the use of abortion became more accepted in Britain over time? Why or why not?

Question 2: How can you account for the high percentages of pregnancies terminated by abortion in the USSR and United States in 1990?

Question 3: Was there a difference in the rate of legal abortions between communist countries and non-communist countries in 1989? Do you think the difference is statistically significant? If so, what factors might explain the difference?

ART INTERPRETATION

Illustration 31.5: The Service Economy (p. 881)

Questions to ponder:

1. How do these scenes contrast with the primarily agricultural working and living environment of seventeenth-century Europe?

2. What are some of the advantages and disadvantages of living in a world where modern technology is so predominant?

3. How effectively does Jacques Tati make his point about technology and modern life?

CHAPTER THIRTY-TWO
EUROPE IN THE AGE OF THE COLD WAR, 1945-75

TABLE ANALYSIS

Table 32.1: Food Production in Postwar Europe (p. 899)

This table lists the quantities of five food staples produced in six European countries for the year 1938, before the start of World War II, and 1945, the last year of the war.

Question 1: What was the average percentage decline in wheat production for all six countries? Which country experienced the greatest percentage decline?

Question 2: Which was the statistically most dangerous country to live in during the war, if you were a cow?

Question 3: What could be the ramifications of such a drastic decline in food production, both during the war and just after the war?

Table 32.2: The German Economic Miracle, 1945-1969 (p. 912)

This table lists the amounts of various products indicative of economic development for Germany for several years between 1949 and 1969.

Question 1: Which product saw the greatest increase between 1949 and 1969?

Question 2: Which product do you think is most indicative of a substantially increased standard of living of the German populace?

Question 3: Compare the 1949 production of iron and coal with the production numbers found in Table 29.1 on page 813. What does the data indicate?

ART INTERPRETATION

Illustration 32.1: Reconstruction of a Devastated Europe (p. 898)

Questions to ponder:

1. How effectively was the devastation of 1945 erased two years later?

2. Where could the money have come from for this reconstruction?

3. How did the rebuilding of bombed cities affect the economy of the city and the country?

CHAPTER THIRTY-THREE
THE NEW BELLE ÉPOQUE: DEMOCRACY AND PROSPERITY SINCE 1975

TABLE ANALYSIS

Table 33.1: Paid Vacations in 1994 (p. 932)

This table gives the average number of days of paid vacation per year for all workers in the given city for the year 1994.

Question 1: In which city did workers receive the largest number of days of paid vacation? The smallest number?

Question 2: Can you draw any conclusions about differences between the United States and Europe regarding paid vacation? Do you think it might have something to do with the power of unions and leftist parties in Europe?

Table 33.2: Taxation in the Late Twentieth Century (p. 932)

This table gives the total taxation as a percentage of GNP and also percentage of taxes from income taxes for five European countries and the United States in the late 1980s. GNP is a measure of the total economic output of a country. Typically, a higher percentage of taxation compared to GNP means a relatively larger government that provides relatively more services for its citizens.

Question 1: Which country took the highest percentage of taxes as a proportion of GNP? Which took the least? Which do you think provides more social welfare programs?

Question 2: Which two countries take the highest percentage of taxes from income taxes?

Question 3: What are the other main sources of taxes besides income taxes?

Table 33.3: The Ethnic Composition of Yugoslavia in 1991 (p. 958)

This table lists the percentages of the various ethnic groups making up Yugoslavia in 1991.

Question 1: Which group made up the largest percentage of Yugoslavia? Did they hold the most power in the country?

Question 2: What were the three largest ethnic groups in Yugoslavia in 1991? How involved were these three groups in the subsequent wars?

ART INTERPRETATION

Illustration 33.1: The Age of Détente (p. 928)

Questions to ponder:

1. What is the overall atmosphere at the memorial?

2. In what ways can Brandt's visit to the memorial be considered diplomacy?

3. Many Germans carry a sense of guilt over World War II, and many non-Germans still harbor substantial resentment toward Germany and Germans because of the war. Do you think Germans should feel any guilt? What about those who were not alive, or were only children, during the war? Has enough time passed for the world to forgive, even while still remembering the lessons?